I0012210

BITWISE ALGORITHMS

DAY BEFORE YOUR CODING INTERVIEW

DCI SERIES

First Edition

Toby Dobrzyniewicz  Ue Kiao 🖐 Aditya Chatterjee

🐾 **OPENGENUS**

BE A NATIONAL PROGRAMMER

INTRODUCTION

This book will change your Bitwise Algorithmic Problem-Solving skills forever. Read it now to level up your future.

This book "**BITWISE ALGORITHMS**" is the only book you need to master bitwise based algorithmic coding problems.

The first chapter is a <u>**CHEATSHEET**</u> for all known Bitwise Algorithmic techniques. This is a goldmine.

Following it, we have covered 4 selected problems which you can complete in a couple of hours. The problems are such that it captures all key ideas of solving a bitwise coding problem and gives a hands-on experience.

With this, you will be able to crack any Coding Interview easily.

After reading this book, you will:

* Master Bitwise tagged algorithmic coding problems and all related problem-solving patterns.
* Clear interviews for full-time positions at high-tech companies (good enough for L3, L4 at Google).

On going through this book, you do not need to solve 100s of problems from Leetcode by spending over a year.

Follow this book, practice the problems and ace every coding interview. Be wise.

We have covered the following:

- Introduction to bitwise algorithms
- Comparing 2 numbers without using comparison
- Reversing a number using bitwise operations
- 2 core coding problems frequently asked in coding interviews

In addition to the explanation of the efficient algorithms to solve the problems, we have covered:

- **C++ Implementations**: So, you can revise your implementation skills and easily implement ideas efficiently.

This book is for:

- Students and developers preparing for Coding Interviews.
- Developers who wanted to tune their skills with Bitwise Algorithms and tricks.
- Students who need a coding sheet for Bitwise Algorithms.

Get started with this book and change the equation of your career.

Book: **Bitwise Algorithms**

Authors (3): Toby Dobrzyniewicz, Aditya Chatterjee, Ue Kiao

About the authors:

Toby Dobrzyniewicz is a Software Developer based in California and originally, from Poland. He has worked at Uber, Palantir and Hitachi over the last decade.

Aditya Chatterjee is an Independent Researcher, Technical Author and the Founding Member of OPENGENUS, a scientific community focused on Computing Technology.

Ue Kiao is a Japanese Software Developer and has played key role in designing systems like TaoBao, AliPay and many more. She has completed her B. Sc in Mathematics and Computing Science at National Taiwan University and PhD at Tokyo Institute of Technology.

Published: September 2024 (Edition 1)

Pages: 80

Publisher: © OpenGenus

ISBN: 9798339776857

Contact: team@opengenus.org

Available on Amazon as Paperback.

Have you observed our cover image?

It has multiple references. Search for *"Modafinil"* and
"0x077CB53111" to understand the cover image better.

Do you love such stories? If so, you should read the short story
book for Programmers FAANGMULA:

TABLE OF CONTENTS

RECOMMENDED BOOKS

DAILY43: Best way to master EASY tagged Coding problems in a month with to-the-point explanation.

No need to practice 1000s of problems over years. This book covers all coding patterns.

Get DAILY43 on Amazon: **amzn.to/4cVoEdK**

- Day before Coding Interview series
- #7daysOfAlgo series

CHEATSHEET: Bitwise Algorithms

Basic bitwise operations

- **AND** (A & B)

A	B	A and B
0	0	0
0	1	0
1	0	0
1	1	1

- **OR** (A || B)

A	B	A or B
0	0	0
0	1	1
1	0	1
1	1	1

- **NOT** (~A)

A	~A
0	1
1	0

- **XOR** (A ^ B)

1

A	B	A xor B
0	0	0
0	1	1
1	0	1
1	1	0

All numbers are represented in binary format in a computing system.

Binary number =	0	1	1	0	1	
Decimal Number =	2^4	2^3	2^2	2^1	2^0	
	16	0	4	0	1	= 21

Left (<<) and right shift (>>)

Left shift by 1: Move all bits by 1 position to the left and add a 0 at the leftmost bit. (**Same as multiplying by 2**).

Right shift by 1: Move all bits by 1 position to the right and add a 0 at the rightmost bit. (**Same as dividing by 2**).

N	0	1	1	0	1
Left shift (N << 1)	1	1	0	1	0
Left shift by 2 (N << 2)	1	0	1	0	0
Right shift by 1 (N >> 1)	0	0	1	1	0

2

Note following **bitwise techniques are valid for integer** data (INT32, INT64, INT8 and other INT variants) only.

For non-integer datatype like float (FP32), different representation is used by differentiating between mantissa and exponent (like IEEE754 for FP32) so bitwise operations are not valid.

Check if number N is odd

The least significant bit will be set to 1 (2^0).

```
N & 1 == true
```

Check if number N is even

The least significant bit will be 0.

```
N & 1 == false
```

Check if two integers have opposite signs

XOR of same bits result in 0. If sign bits are opposite, resultant number will be negative.

3

```
if (x^y > 0)
    return false;
else
    return true;
```

Add 1 to a given number

```
(-(~x))
```

Multiply a number by 2

```
X << 1
```

Divide a number by 2

```
X >> 1
```

Set the lowest significant set bit to 0

```
X & (X - 1)
```

Return the lowest significant set bit only (other bits as 0)

```
X & ~(X - 1)
```

Return the MOST significant set bit only (other bits as 0)

For 32-bits:

```c
uint32_t keepHighestSetBit(uint32_t N)
{
    N |= (N >>  1);
    N |= (N >>  2);
    N |= (N >>  4);
    N |= (N >>  8);
    N |= (N >> 16);
    return N - (N >> 1);
}
```

Find the middle element without overflow

```c
int L = 2e9, R = 2e9+4;
int mid = (L + R) / 2;          // overflow
int mid = (L&R) + ((L^R) >> 1); // correct
```

Fast minimum and maximum

This works assuming x-y does not underflow or overflow.

```
#define max(x, y) (y-x >> 31 & (x^y) ^ y)
#define min(x, y) (y-x >> 31 & (x^y) ^ x)
```

Compute modulus division by a power of 2

```
X % (2^N)
= X & (1 << N - 1);
```

Rotate bits of a number by K position

```
int leftCircularShift(int x, int K)
    return (x << K) | (x >> K);

int rightCircularShift(int x, int K)
    return (x >> K) | (x << K);
```

Built-in functions in GCC for bitwise operations:

- Count number of set (1) bits

```
__builtin_popcount(N)
```

- Return 1 if N has odd number of set bits or else 0

```
__builtin_parity(N)
```

- Count number of leading zeros (from left side)

```
__builtin_clz(N)
```

- Count number of trailing zeros (from right)

```
__builtin_ctz(N)
```

- Find First Set: Index of the least significant set bit (from right)

```
__builtin_ffs(N)
```

Built-in functions in Standard C library

- Find index of first set bit

```
#include <strings.h>
int index = ffs(N);
```

Check whether a given number is a power of 4

```
if ( !(x & (x-1)) ) {
    if(__builtin_ctz(x) % 2 == 0)
        return true;
```

Count number of bits to be flipped to convert A to B

```
__builtin_popcount(a ^ b);
```

Find whether a number is power of two

```
return (N > 0 and !(N & (N-1)));
```

Position of Least significant set bit

For 32-bit number using De Bruijn Sequence:

```
unsigned int v;  // 32-bit number
int r; // position of least significant set
bit
static const int
MultiplyDeBruijnBitPosition[32] =
{
```

8

```
   0, 1, 28, 2, 29, 14, 24, 3, 30, 22, 20,
15, 25, 17, 4, 8,
   31, 27, 13, 23, 21, 19, 16, 7, 26, 12,
18, 6, 11, 5, 10, 9
};
r =
MultiplyDeBruijnBitPosition[((uint32_t)((v
& -v) * 0x077CB531U)) >> 27];
```

This works as:

- (v & -v) returns a number with only the least significant bit set.
- Multiplying with 0x077CB531U results in a **hash value** from 0 to 31.
- The number 0x077CB531U is a DeBruijn sequence. The table MultiplyDeBruijnBitPosition is a lookup table that maps the multiplication with the DeBruijn sequence with the correct output.

Position of rightmost set bit

ffs() is a built-in function in C++ that returns the position of the first (least significant) bit set. It is in <string.h>

```
ffs(x);
//another approach
log2(x & -x) + 1;
//another approach
if (x != 0)
    __builtin_ctz(x)+1;
```

Calculate XOR from 1 to N

```
switch(n & 3) // n % 4
{
    case 0: return n;
    case 1: return 1;
    case 2: return n + 1;
    case 3: return 0;
}
```

This works as:

- If N is even, then **N XOR (N+1) = 1**.
- There are Floor((N+1)/2) pairs with above
  property for 1 to N.
  - (0,1) (2,3), (4,5), ...
  - N can be left out at the end.
  - Note the 1s from these pairs are XORed
    with each other again.

Binary representation of a given number

```
void bin(unsigned n)
{
    if (n > 1)
        bin(n>>1);

    cout << (d & 1) << endl;
}
```

Find position of only set bit

```
if(!(n&(n-1)))
        ffs(n);
```

Turn off a particular bit in a number

```
x & (~1<<(pos-1));
```

Check if 2 numbers are equal

```
if ((x ^ y))
    return false;
else
    return true;
```

Find XOR of numbers without using XOR operator

```
(x | y) & (~x | ~y);
```

Swap two variables

```
x = x ^ y;
y = x ^ y;
x = x ^ y;
```

Swap three variables

```
x = x ^ y ^ z;
y = x ^ y ^ z;
z = x ^ y ^ z;
x = x ^ y ^ z;
```

Toggle Kth bit of a number

Toggle K^{th} bit of a number

```
x = x ^ 1<<(k-1);
```

Toggle all bits except Kth bit of a number

```
x = ~(x ^ 1<<(k-1);)
```

Set the rightmost unset bit

```
x = x | (x+1)
```

Toggle the last m bits

```
x ^ ~(-1<<m)
```

Maximum XOR-value of at-most k-elements from 1 to N

```
int x = log2(n) + 1;
return x<<1 - 1;

//Alt way

int res = 1;
while (res <= n)
    res <<= 1;
// Finding number greater than
// or equal to n with most significant
// bit same as n. For example, if n is
// 4, result is 7. If n is 5 or 6, result
// is 7
```

13

```
// Return res - 1 which denotes
// a number with all bits set to 1
return res - 1;
```

Check if a number is divisible by 8 using bitwise operators

```
return (((N >> 3) << 3) == N);
```

Toggle bits of a number except first and last bits

```
int size = sizeof(int)*8 -
__builtin_clz(n);
int one = (1<<(size-1))-1;
n = n ^ one;
n = n ^ 1;
```

Toggle all even bits of a number

```
int temp = n,i=1;
while(temp){
    n = n ^ 1>>(i*2);
    i++;
    temp = temp>>1;
}
```

Brian Kernighan's Algorithm for counting set Bits

```
while(n) {
    n &=(n-1);
    count++;
}
```

INTRODUCTION TO BITWISE OPERATIONS

There are 3 fundamental operations namely:

- AND
- OR
- NOT

All other bitwise operations can be created using these 3 bitwise operations. To facilitate bitwise operations, computing system support these 3 bitwise operations as well:

- XOR
- LEFT SHIFT
- RIGHT SHIFT

Bitwise AND (&)

This operator preforms a binary AND operation between the two operands. This means it compares the bits individually, the resultant bit mapping to 1 or true only if both bits fed to it are 1 as well.

Truth table:

A	B	A and B
0	0	0
0	1	0
1	0	0
1	1	1

Example:

	Input 1: 15	1	1	1	1
Bitwise AND (&)	Input 2: 9	1	0	0	1
	Result	1	0	0	1

Bitwise OR (|)

This operator preforms a binary OR operation; the resultant bit mapping to 1 if one or more of the inputs to it is 1.

Truth table:

A	B	A or B
0	0	0
0	1	1
1	0	1
1	1	1

Example:

	Input 1: 15	1	1	1	1
Bitwise OR (|)	Input 2: 9	1	0	0	1
	Result	1	1	1	1

Bitwise XOR (^)

Performs the exclusive-OR or XOR operation; the resultant bit maps to 1 if both inputs have even number of ones (i.e. 0-1 or 1-0) but 0 otherwise.

Truth table:

A	B	A xor B
0	0	0
0	1	1
1	0	1
1	1	0

Example:

	Input 1: 15	1	1	1	1
Bitwise XOR (^)	Input 2: 9	1	0	0	1
	Result	0	1	1	0

Bitwise Unary NOT (~)

Performs complementation or negation operation; inverts all the bits of the number, i.e. 0->1 and 1->0.

Truth table:

A	~A
0	1
1	0

Unary NOT (~)	Input (13)	1	1	0	1
	Result	0	0	1	0

Left Shift (<<)

Performs a shift or rotation by a specified number of positions. Every bit is moved left M positions. Further, the MSB (Most Significant Bit) is shifted to the LSB (Least Significant Bit) for every rotation. It is the equivalent of multiplying the number by 2 M times that is 2^M.

Example:

Left Shift (<<)	Input (7)	0	1	1	1
	Result (14)	1	1	1	0

19

Right Shift (>>)

Every bit is moved right n positions. Further, in case of signed 2's complement numbers, the sign bit is moved into the MSB position. It is the equivalent of dividing the number by 2 M times that is 2^M.

Example:

Right Shift (<<)	Input (14)	1	1	1	0
	Result (7)	0	1	1	1

Integer representation

All numbers are represented in binary format.

Integers are computed by adding powers of 2 for each corresponding set bit.

Bit pattern	1	1	0	0	1	1	1	0	0
Bit index	8	7	6	5	4	3	2	1	0
Power of 2	2^8	2^7	2^6	2^5	2^4	2^3	2^2	2^1	2^0

Take the sum of powers of 2 for every corresponding set bit:

$2^2 + 2^3 + 2^4 + 2^7 + 2^8$

$= 4 + 8 + 16 + 128 + 256$

$= 412$

So, the bit pattern represents 412.

Similarly, all integers are represented.

In practice, there are different forms of integers and all follow the same bit pattern format:

- INT4 : Integers using 4 bits
- INT32 : Integers using 32 bits
- INT64 : Integers using 64 bits

And so on.

Note this is not valid for floating point numbers as it involve:

- Two components: one for the fractional part and other for the integer part (power of 2).
- Numbers are first represented in scientific notation.

- There are custom rules for each format.

There are different floating formats:

- FLOAT32: IEEE 754 format
- BFLOAT16
- FP8: Multiple variants in FP8 like E5M3, E4M4 and more.

And so on.

Why Bitwise algorithms needed?

Computers understand bits and all programs are converted to binary format after multiple compiler phases.

All arithmetic operations can be done using bitwise operations (this is valid for floating point numbers as well by considering the custom rules).

Computers have bitwise operations as **highly optimized operations**.

Having an insight on how to perform a computation using bitwise operations will enable a programmer to unlock significant performance optimizations.

Using bitwise operations give a strong intuition of all numbers are represented and how computations are performed.

PROBLEM 1: Compare 2 numbers

In this chapter, we will explore the concept of performing arithmetic comparisons (equal, larger, smaller) through bitwise operations.

Sub-topics:

- Check if both operands are equal
- Check which operand is smaller/ larger in value
- Time and Space Complexity

What if you have two compare two operands without using the comparison operator directly?

Comparisons can be performed without the use of the comparison operator. We will be comparing two operands to check for the following cases:

- Check if both operands are equal
- Check which operand is smaller/larger in value

Check if both operands are equal

We can check if two given values are equal or not by making use of the **XOR operator**. If two numbers are equal, then their bitwise XOR will always result in **0**.

For example:

In decimal form, **a = 9** and **b = 9**

In binary form, **a = 1001** and **b = 1001**

a ^ b = 1001 ^ 1001

a ^ b = 0000

a ^ b = 0 (in decimal form)

Therefore, a = b.

Code example in C++:

```cpp
#include <iostream>
using namespace std;

bool bitCheckEqual(int x, int y) {
    return !(x ^ y);
}

int main() {
    cout << boolalpha << bitCheckEqual(16,
61) << endl;
    return 0;
}
```

The above code generates the following output.

```
False
```

The code is very simple and does what it is supposed to do, however, keep in mind that you can only share integer values to the bitCheckEqual() function, else you will encounter an error as **bitwise operations are supported for integer values only**.

Check which operand is smaller/larger in value

We can check which number is smaller or larger by performing the following steps:

- Use the XOR operator on both the given values to find out the **bits that differ** among them.
- Now, we have to determine the **most significant bits (MSB) that differ** (MSBs are the bits that are present at the left-most side of a given number). This can be done by using the bitwise OR bitwise and Right Shift operators.

26

- Perform a check to see as to which operand does the MSB belong to.
- Depending upon this check, return the final answer. If a value does not contain the MSB, then it is the smaller value and we can simply return it, else return the other value as there is no other alternative. This operation can be performed by using the **bitwise AND** and **bitwise XOR** operators.

Step by step example:

In decimal form, a = 9 & b = 5

In binary form, a = 1001 & b = 101

Let MSB = a ^ b

MSB = 1001 ^ 101

∴ MSB = 1100

It is clear that the bits differ at two places.

Now let us determine the first MSB bit.

MSB = MSB | (MSB >> 1)

MSB = 1100 | (1100 >> 1)

MSB = 1100 | 110

MSB = 1110

∴ MSB = 14 (in decimal form)

We will repeat the same steps and update the value by which we are performing the right shift on MSB by 2, 4, 8 and 16.

Performing these steps, we get the final value of MSB as 1111 (in binary) and 15 (in decimal).

Now we have to reduce the value of MSB by right shifting MSB by 1 and then subtracting it from itself.

Now, MSB = MSB - (MSB >> 1)

MSB = 1111 - (1111 >> 1)

MSB = 1111 - 111

MSB = 1000

∴ MSB = 8 (in decimal form)

Now perform the bitwise AND operation between any of the two given values with MSB and then perform XOR of that value with MSB. Depending upon the value that comes out from this operation, return the final answer to the user.

For the sake of our example, let us perform the AND operation between MSB and y and then use XOR between that value and MSB itself.

(b & MSB) ^ MSB

(101 & 1000) ^ 1000

0 ^ 1000

1000 = 8 (in decimal form)

Since the value is not 0, that means that b is the smaller value of the two numbers, so we can simply return b as our final answer.

To find out the larger value of the two numbers, we can simply flip the condition and return the value of a.

Code example in C++:

```cpp
#include <iostream>
using namespace std;

int bitCheckLess(int x, int y) {
    int msb = x ^ y;
    msb |= (msb >> 1);
    msb |= (msb >> 2);
    msb |= (msb >> 4);
    msb |= (msb >> 8);
    msb |= (msb >> 16);
    msb = msb - (msb >> 1);
    return (y & msb) == msb ? x : y;
}

int main() {
    cout << bitCheckLess(9, 5) << endl;
    return 0;
}
```

The above code generates the following output.

```
5
```

For finding the larger value, the code will be similar except for the if condition part. Code example in C++:

```cpp
#include <iostream>
using namespace std;

int bitCheckLarge(int x, int y) {
    int msb = x ^ y;
    msb |= (msb >> 1);
    msb |= (msb >> 2);
    msb |= (msb >> 4);
    msb |= (msb >> 8);
    msb |= (msb >> 16);
    msb = msb - (msb >> 1);
    return (y & msb) == msb ? y : x;
}

int main() {
    cout << bitCheckLarge(12314, 12315) <<
endl;
    return 0;
}
```

The above code generates the following output.

```
12315
```

Once again, both the codes do what they are supposed to do, albeit they use considerably more operations than our previous algorithm. Keep in mind that you can only share integer values to the bitCheckLess() and bitCheckLarge() functions, else you will encounter an error as bitwise operations are generally supported for whole integer values only.

Time and Space Complexity

Time complexity: The comparisons being performed in the comparison function depends upon the **number of bits** that the input number has. Although bitwise operations are considerably faster, this would make the overall time complexity of our algorithm to be O(M), where M = number of bits in the input number.

For a given number N, there are O(logN) bits in N so M = O(logN).

Space complexity: No extra space is being used other than the msb variable, hence the overall space complexity of our algorithm will be O(1).

PROBLEM 2: Reverse number

Given a 32-bit integer, reverse the bits and get the equivalent number.

Example: Input: **5** = 0000 0000 0000 0000 0000 0000 0000 **0101**

Reversed = **1010** 0000 0000 0000 0000 0000 0000 0000 = **2684354560**

<u>Solution</u>:

The first approach is to reverse the bits natively by handling one bit at a time. The first approach is:

- Create a new 32-bit number initialized to 0.
- Loop through all bits of the original number from right to left.
  - o Shift the new number to left by one position.
  - o By shifting, we moved previous bits to left (partial reversal). Think of doing this N times.
  - o If current bit is 1, add 1 to the above new number and update it.
- Resultant number is reversed bitwise.

Another approach in C++ is to use bitset which allows us to treat the binary representation of a number as an array. The core idea is same as the previous approach but implementation is simplified using two pointer approach.

- Create bitset for the integer.
- Traverse the bitset array using two pointers: one from front and other from end.
  - Swap both pointers at each step.

The third approach is to use an insightful bitwise trick. This approach is a neat **advanced trick** and is O(1) time solution as bitwise operations take O(1) time internally.

- Swap the first 16 bits with the last 16 bits as 2 blocks.
- Swap 8 bits as blocks within the above 2 blocks of 16 bits.
  - (n & 11111111000000001111111100000000) = Extracts the first 8 bits in the 2 16-bit blocks. See the first 8 bits are set to 1 so a bitwise AND extracts the required data.

- o The hexadecimal representation of
  1111111100000000**11111111**00000000
  is 0xff00ff00.
- o Similarly, (n & 0x00ff00ff) extracts the
  last 8 bits in each 16-bit blocks.
- Next, swap 4 bits as blocks within the 4 blocks
  of size 8 bits.
- Finally, swap 2 bits as blocks within the 8
  blocks of size 4 bits.

The resultant binary number is reversed. You can
use the binary numbers or the corresponding
hexadecimal numbers.

This algorithm is used internally in Integer.reverse
method of Java's JDK.

Complexity:

Assume there are N bits in the number.

- Native reversal:
  - o Time complexity: O(N)
  - o Space complexity: O(N)
- Reversal using bitset:
  - o Time complexity: O(N)
  - o Space complexity: O(N)
- Reversal using bitwise trick:

- o Time complexity: O(1)
- o Space complexity: O(1)

C++ code snippet for traversal approach:

```cpp
// Traversal and reversal together
uint32_t reverseBits(uint32_t n) {
    uint32_t result= 0;
    int i = 0;
    for(; i<32; ++i)
        // Right to left reading
        // Add current bit and move entire
number to left
        result = (result<<1) + (n>>i & 1);
    return result;
}
```

C++ code snippet using two pointer approach using bitset:

```cpp
// Two pointer swap approach
uint32_t reverseBits(uint32_t n) {
    bitset<32> bs{n};
    int left{0}, right{31};
    while(left < right) {
        // Swap
        bool tmp = bs[left];
        bs[left++] = bs[right];
        bs[right--] = tmp;
    }
    return bs.to_ulong();
```

```
}
```

C++ code snippet:

```
// Reverse bits in 32-bit number
uint32_t reverseBits(uint32_t n) {
    n = (n >> 16) | (n << 16);
    n = ((n & 0xff00ff00) >> 8) | ((n &
0x00ff00ff) << 8);
    n = ((n & 0xf0f0f0f0) >> 4) | ((n &
0x0f0f0f0f) << 4);
    n = ((n & 0xcccccccc) >> 2) | ((n &
0x33333333) << 2);
    n = ((n & 0xaaaaaaaa) >> 1) | ((n &
0x55555555) << 1);
    return n;
}
```

C++ code snippet for the same bitwise approach but using bit mask instead of hexadecimal numbers:

```
uint32_t reverseBits(uint32_t n) {
    n = (n >> 16) | (n << 16);
    n = ((n &
0b11111111000000001111111100000000) >> 8) |
((n & 0b00000000111111110000000011111111)
<< 8);
```

37

```
    n = ((n &
0b11110000111100001111000011110000) >> 4) |
((n & 0b00001111000011110000111100001111)
<< 4);
    n = ((n &
0b11001100110011001100110011001100) >> 2) |
((n & 0b00110011001100110011001100110011)
<< 2);
    n = ((n &
0b10101010101010101010101010101010) >> 1) |
((n & 0b01010101010101010101010101010101)
<< 1);
    return n;
}
```

PROBLEM 3: XOR of array = 0

You are given an array of N positive integers. Your task is to find the minimum number of operations to make XOR of array equal to zero. Allowed operations are defined as follows:

- The operation that can be performed are increment or decrement by one.
- Select the element on which you will perform the operation. Note that all the operations must be performed only on the selected element.

Example

```
Input:
Number of elements in array = 3
Elements = 2 4 7

Output:
1
```

Explanation: We will decrement 7 to 6 and then the XOR of all the elements is zero. This involve 1 decrement operation.

```
Input:
Number of elements in array = 4
Elements = 5 5 4 4

Output:
0
```

Explanation: XOR of an element with itself is zero.

Explanation of solution

Before discussing the various approaches to the problem, let us briefly review XOR.

XOR (also known as **exclusive-or**) of two one-bit number is defined by the following table:

A	B	A xor B
0	0	0
0	1	1
1	0	1
1	1	0

XOR of two multiple-bit numbers is simply the XOR of the corresponding individual bits.

Example: The XOR of 5 (101 in binary) and 6 (110 in binary) will be 011 in binary or 3 in decimal.

Property of XOR: XOR of two numbers can be zero only when both the numbers are equal.

We can solve this problem by two approaches:

- Brute force approach
- Optimized approach

Brute force approach:

The core idea is to check the number of operations needed to change all elements individually such that the XOR of all elements is 0 and maintain the minimum number of operations.

Steps:

- Process all N elements one by one.
- For the current element, compute the XOR of all other N-1 elements.
  - ○ If the XOR is same as the current element, no operation need to be

performed as the XOR of all N elements will be 0.

- o Else, number of operations = Absolute value of Current element – XOR of other N-1 elements.
- Find the minimum number of operations across all N elements. This is the answer.

Complexity:

- Time Complexity: **O(N²)**
- Space Complexity: O(1)

EXAMPLE: Let us find the answer when the elements of array are 2, 4 ,7 and 8. Now we need to find the minimum number of changes to one element so that XOR of the array is zero.

Let us assume that selected number is 2. Then we must change 2 to become equal to 4 XOR 7 XOR 8 i.e. 11. Operations for 2 are equal to 9. Similarly, operations for 4, 7 and 8 are equal to 9, 7 and 7 respectively.

Answer is equal to minimum(9,9,7,7) that is 7.

Optimized approach:

The brute force approach can be optimized by considering 3 properties of XOR operation:

- It is associative.
- XOR of an element with itself is zero.
- XOR of a number with zero is the number itself.

The above behavior implies an important behavior of XOR that is if $M = a \wedge b$ ($\wedge$ is XOR, a and b are integers) then, $M \wedge b$ will be equal to **a**.

Now with this property in hand, we will make the process of finding the XOR of all elements excluding the ith element **O(1)** time. In the brute force approach, this takes **O(N)** time.

First, we will find XOR of all the elements of the array and store it in a variable (say A).

Then to find the XOR of all the elements excluding the ith element, we will do XOR(A, array[i]). Thus the number of increment/decrement operations for the ith element will be **absolute(array[i]-XOR(A, array[i]))**.

We will calculate the cost for each element of the array and the minimum of these costs will be the answer.

EXAMPLE:

Let us find the answer when the array is:

2, 4, 7, 8

Now we need to find the minimum number of changes to one element so that XOR of the array is zero. Let us find the XOR of the whole array and store it in a variable

M. M = 2 XOR 4 XOR 7 XOR 8 i.e. M = 9.

Let us assume that selected number is 2. Then we must change 2 to become equal to M XOR 2

(XOR of all numbers excluding two) that is 11. So, operations for 2 are equal to 9. Similarly, operations for 4, 7 and 8 are equal to 9, 7 and 7 respectively (We will run a loop over the array for this). Answer is equal to **minimum(9,9,7,7) i.e. 7**.

C++ implementation:

44

```cpp
#include <iostream>
#include <climits>
#include <cmath>
using namespace std;

//function definition
int minxor(int matrix[], int length){
        int answer=INT_MAX,obtainedxor=0;
        for(int i=0;i<length;++i){
                obtainedxor^=matrix[i];
        }

        int cost;
        for(int i=0;i<length;++i){

        cost=abs((obtainedxor^matrix[i])-
matrix[i]);
                if(answer>cost){
                        answer=cost;
                }
        }

        return answer;
}

int main(){
        //input
        int length;
        cout<<"No. of elements in array =
";
        cin>>length;
        int matrix[length];
        cout<<"Elements = ";
        for(int i=0;i<length;++i){
```

```
            cin>>matrix[i];
    }

    //output
    cout<<minxor(matrix, length)<<"\n";
    return 0;
}
```

Time Complexity

- Worst case time complexity: O(N)
- Average case time complexity: Θ(N)
- Best case time complexity: Ω(N)
- Auxiliary space: O(1)

where N is the number of elements

PROBLEM 4: Nearest smaller and greater numbers

In this chapter, we will explore the various ways we can find the Nearest smaller and greater numbers with same number of set bits for given number.

We will explore two approaches:

- The brute force approach
- The Bit manipulation

Sub-topics:

- Understanding the problem
- Brute-force approach
- Time Complexity for this approach
- Bit manipulation approach
- Nearest Greater Number
- Nearest Lesser Number
- Time Complexity

Let us get started!

Understanding the problem

Suppose we are given a number, say **103**. We need to find the nearest smaller and greater numbers which have the same number of set bits that is '1' bits in their binary representation.

For nearest greater number, we have

```
103 = 1 1 0 0 1 1 1
104 = 1 1 0 1 0 0 0
105 = 1 1 0 1 0 0 1
106 = 1 1 0 1 0 1 0
107 = 1 1 0 1 0 1 1
```

We see that **107** has the same number of set bits as 103. So, 107 is the nearest greater number with the same set bits as 103.

Similarly, to find the nearest smaller number with the same number of set bits, we can go backwards. We will arrive at **94** whose binary representation is -

```
94 = 1 0 1 1 1 1 0
```

103, 107 and 94- all have 5 set bits. Let us see how we can solve this problem.

Brute-force approach

The core idea is to increment the original number one by one and check if it has the same number of set bits. The first number to satisfy the condition is the nearest greater number.

Similarly, for the nearest smaller number, decrement the original number one by one and check accordingly.

Steps:

- N = original number with M set bits
- Increment N one by one
  - If current number K has M set bits, K is the nearest greater number.
- Decrement N one by one.
  - If current number K has M set bits, K is the nearest smaller number.

Implementation

In C++, we need a couple of functions to get this done. Let us see these one by one:

- The count1() function takes in a number as parameter and returns the number of set '1' bits in it. We do this by **AND**ing the last bit with 1 to check if it is 1, and then we do a left shift on the number. This goes on while the number is not 0.

```cpp
int count1(int n)
{
    int ones=0;
    while(n){
        if(n&1==1){
            ones++;
        }
        n=n>>1;
    }
    return ones;
}
```

- The nearestgreater()/nearestlesser() function. nearestlesser() and nearestgreater() take in a integer parameter and decrement/ increment iteratively and check the number of set bits. When the answer is found, the loop is broken and the value is returned.

```
int nearestgreater(int n){
    int m=n+1;
    int base=count1(n);
    while(m) {
     if(count1(m)==base){
         return m;
     }
     m++;
    }
}

int nearestlesser(int n){
    int m=n-1;
    int base=count1(n);
    while(m){
     if(count1(m)==base){
         return m;
     }
     m--;
    }
}
```

Complete C++ implementation of the brute force
approach:

```
#include <bits/stdc++.h>
using namespace std;

int count1(int n)
{
    int one=0;
```

```
    while(n){
        if(n&1==1){
            one++;
        }
        n=n>>1;
    }
    return one;
}

int nearestgreater(int n){
    int m=n+1;
    int base=count1(n);
    while(m){
     if(count1(m)==base){
         return m;
     }
     m++;
    }
}

int nearestlesser(int n){
    int m=n-1;
    int base=count1(n);
    while(m){
     if(count1(m)==base){
         return m;
     }
     m--;
    }
}

int main()
{
    int i=103,j=107;
    int m=nearestgreater(i);
```

```
    cout<<m<<" "<<count1(m)<<endl;
    int p=nearestlesser(j);
    cout<<p<<" "<<count1(p);
    return 0;
}
```

We get the following output:

```
107 5
103 5
```

Time Complexity for brute force approach

The brute force approach has **O(N logN)** time
complexity, since it iterates over and over until a
possible answer is found, and for every iteration,
it checks the number of set bits using a function
call.

Since, number of bits in a number N is $\log_2 N+1$, so
time complexity of count1() is *O(log n)*.
An iterative call will make the overall time
complexity *O(nlog n)*.

The maximum number of cases to be checked will
be N as in the worst case, all the bits need to be
shifted for the larger/ smaller number.

Bit manipulation approach

In this approach, we will use a few bitwise operators to find the nearest greater and smaller number with the same number of set bits. This will require a bit-by-bit analysis of numbers on our end to see what changes we must make to solve our problem.

Nearest Greater Number

We have the number **103 (1 1 0 0 1 1 1)**, and the nearest greater number **107 (1 1 0 1 0 1 1)**.

Now, for any number, since we need to maintain the same number of set bits and yet, increase the value, we will need to:

- change a zero bit to one
- counter this by turning a different one bit to zero.

Our **first observation** should be that the number will only increase if the zero-to-one transition happens to the left of the one-to-zero transition.

That is, the 8-bit must change from zero to one if we want to increase the number after switching the 4-bit from one to zero.

Our **second observation** is that we are looking for the *nearest* greater number. So, we cannot just switch any random left zero to one and a right one to zero. We must ensure that the **increase in value is minimal**.

This can be achieved by scanning the bits right to left and selecting the first zero bit which has a one bit on its immediate right.

Observe this:

				C			
103	1	1	0	0	1	1	1
Bit index	6	5	4	3	2	1	0

The rightmost zero with a one to the right of it is present at index 3. (Please note that we begin indexing from 0.)

So, we switch the 0 bit to 1 and end up temporarily with this: 1 1 0 **1** 1 1

Now, we need to counter this move by changing one of the set bits on the right to 0. Since the increase must be minimal, all the bits on the right of the changed bit (say position C) must be arranged in the manner where they form the most minimum number. That is, the 0's must come in the higher indexes and the 1's must come at the lower ones. We shall also switch a set bit to 0.

Let us take a different example to make this even clearer:

				C					
412	1	1	0	0	1	1	1	0	0
Bit index	8	7	6	5	4	3	2	1	0

The zero bit we pick is at index 5.

Now, we must rearrange the bits to the right of C to giving the overall number a minimal increment. So, we arrange the zeroes first and then, the ones. We also change one set bit to 0.

So, we get:

				C					
412	1	1	0	0	1	1	1	0	0
Bit index	8	7	6	5	4	3	2	1	0

NEW = 419	1	1	0	1	0	0	0	1	1

So, we have now understood what we need to do. Let us see how we can use bitwise operators to accomplish this.

First, we shall find the position of zero bit which we must change to one. Here, C=5.

As we look for this zero bit, we count the number of 0 and 1 bits on the way. Let count0 be the number of zeroes and count1 be the number of ones. Here, count0=2 and count1=3. Note that C=count0+count1.

Now, we set the right bits to the sequence of (count0) + 1 zero bits and (count1)-1 one bits, i.e. in this case 3 zeroes followed by 2 ones: 0 0 0 1 1. This can be done as follows:

```
int nearestgreater(int n)
```

```
{
        int tempvar = n;
        int count0 = 0;
        int count1 = 0;

        while (((tempvar & 1) == 0) &&
(tempvar != 0))
        {
                count0 ++;
                tempvar >>= 1;
        }
        while ((tempvar & 1)==1)
        {
                count1++;
                tempvar >>= 1;
        }

        if (count0 +count1 == 31 || count0
+count1== 0)
                return -1;

         int C = count0 + count1; //1

        n |= (1 << C); //2

        n &= ~((1 << C) - 1); //3

        n |= (1 << (count1 - 1)) - 1; //4

        return n;
}
```

In this function:

- The two while loops analyze the bits from the right and stop at the point where bit is 0 with 1 on its right.
- If all the bits are 0 or 1, then, return -1 and exit.
- We need to set the bit at position C. So, take a new 1 bit and shift it leftwards by C steps. So, the the number begins 1 0 0 0 0 0...(C-1 zeroes). This number is OR'ed with the given number. Since any bit OR'ed with 1 is 1, so we have set our bit at the required index.
- Next, we set all the bits after Cth bit as 0.

For this, we take (1<<C). Example:

```
C=5
count0=2
count1=3
So, suppose x=(1<<C)=1 0 0 0 0 0.
```

Since we aim to turn all the right bits to 0, would a direct AND with 1<<C do the trick?

I don't think so.

Absolutely!

A direct AND with 1<<C is useless as we know that int objects are 32 bits long.

So, when we write 10000, the one bit actually has a lot of zeroes on its left. We don't mention them because they add no value to the number. So, if we directly AND n with 1<<C, all the bits in n to the left of position C will get AND'ed with 0 and turn 0.

So, let us work around this.

```
x=(1<<C)=1 0 0 0 0 0.
Subtracting 1 from x, we get
x-1=0 1 1 1 1 1
Now, negating this, we have
~(x-1)=1 1 1 1 1 1 1 1 1 1 1 1 1 1 1 1
1 1 1 1 1 1 1 1 1 1 1 1 0 0 0 0 0.

So, when we AND this with n, all the
bits AND'ed with 0 turn 0. The rest r
emain unaffected.
```

Now that every bit on the right of C position is set to 0, we shall set the last count1-1 bits to 1. We do this as follows:

```
y=1<<(Count1-1)= 1<<2 = 100.
Negating y,
We get y=011.
We OR n with y to get the required bi
ts set as needed.
So, n= 1  1  0  1  0  0  0  1  1.
```

Thus, we have arrived at our desired number.

Nearest Lesser Number

This approach is similar to the above approach. Suppose we have the number 419=110100011. Now, we need to find the nearest lesser number with the same number of bits. For this, we look for the rightmost 1 bit which has a 0 in its immediate right.

We count the number of zeroes and ones on the way and store it in count0 and count1. Then, this 1 bit is switched to 0 to reduce the value of n.

Now, we must counter this step by turning a 0 bit to 1 on the right side of the position C. We also manipulate the bits to the right of C to make sure the difference is minimal.

This involves adding all the 1 bits before the 0 bits. Let us see how this can be done in code:

```
int nearestlesser(int n)
{
    int tempvar = n;
    int count0 = 0;
    int count1= 0;

    while ((tempvar & 1) == 1)
    {
        count1++;
        tempvar = tempvar >> 1;
    }

    if (tempvar == 0)
        return -1;

    while (((tempvar & 1) == 0) &&
(tempvar!= 0))
    {
        count0++;
        tempvar  = tempvar >> 1;
    }
```

```
    int C = count0 + count1; //1

    n = n & ((~0) << (C + 1)); //2

    int dummy = (1 << (count1 + 1)) -
1; //3

    n = n | dummy << (count0 - 1);
//4

    return n;
}
```

First, we use two while loops to find count of 0 and 1 bits. This is stored in count0 and count1. When we find the first 1 bit with a 0 on the right, the counting stops. Here, count0=3 and count1=2. So, C=5.

Now, once we find the bit we need to change to 0, we set about to do just that.

```
                    C
Here, n=1 1 0 1 0 0 0 1 1.
```

An obvious question would be- *aren't 1 and ~0 the same thing?* Like earlier, we know that int objects have 32 bits. So, ~0 is actually 1 1 1 1 1 ...32 times, and no just 1.

Now, we need to reset all the bits at C and post C. So, we left shift ~0 C+1 times.
So,

```
~0<<(C+1)=~0<<6=111111111111111111
11111111000000
```

When we AND this with n, all the bits on and after C turn 0. All the other bits remain unchanged.

Now, from index 0 to C-1, we need to add count1+1 one bits and count0-1 zero bits, in that order. We take a dummy variable.

Here, count1=2. So, we need to add an extra one to balance the number of set bits. So,

```
1<<(Count1+1)=1<<3=1000.
Subtracting 1, we get

1<<(Count1+1)-1=0111. So, dummy=01
11.
```

It may appear that negating 1000 can also yield 0111. But, it doesn't. You know why.

After the 0111, we also need to add count0-1 zeroes. This can easily be done using a left shift.

```
dummy<<(count0-1)=011100.
Now, at this stage, n=1 1 0 0 0 0
0 0 0.
```

So, OR'ing n with dummy<<(count0-1), we get n=110011100= 412, which is the required answer.

So, taking an overall look at the code:

```
#include <bits/stdc++.h>
using namespace std;
```

```
int nearestgreater(int n)
{

        int tempvar = n;
        int count0 = 0;
        int count1 = 0;

        while (((tempvar & 1) == 0) &&
(tempvar != 0))
        {
                count0 ++;
                tempvar >>= 1;
        }
        while ((tempvar & 1)==1)
        {
                count1++;
                tempvar >>= 1;
        }

        if (count0 +count1 == 31 ||
count0 +count1== 0)
                return -1;

        int C = count0 + count1; //1

        n |= (1 << C); //2

        n &= ~((1 << C) - 1); //3
```

```
         n |= (1 << (count1 - 1)) - 1;
//4


     return n;
}
int nearestlesser(int n)
{
    int tempvar = n;
    int count0 = 0;
    int count1= 0;

    while ((tempvar & 1) == 1)
    {
        count1++;
        tempvar = tempvar >> 1;
    }

    if (tempvar == 0)
        return -1;

    while (((tempvar & 1) == 0) &&
(tempvar!= 0))
    {
        count0++;
        tempvar  = tempvar >> 1;
    }

    int C = count0 + count1; //1

    n = n & ((~0) << (C + 1)); //2
```

```
    int dummy = (1 << (count1 + 1)) -
1;  //3

    n = n | dummy << (count0 - 1);
//4

    return n;
}
int main()
{
    int n = 412;  // input 1
    cout << nearestgreater(n) <<
endl;
    n=419;
    cout << nearestlesser(n)<<endl;
    return 0;
}
```

Time Complexity

- Time Complexity: **O(logN)**
- Space Complexity: **O(1)**

Since this method uses 2 while loops followed by a set of constant operations. The two while loops traverse the bits of the given number. Since every number N has **log₂N + 1 bits**. So, time complexity of the while loops= $O(\log n)+O(\log n)=O(\log n)$.

Time complexity of the operations: $O(1)$.
So, overall complexity is $O(\log n)+O(1)=O(\log n)$.

CONCLUDING NOTE

As a next step, you may randomly pick a problem from our Bitwise cheatsheet, read the problem statement and dive into designing your own solution and implement it in a Programming Language of your choice.

Remember, we are here to help you. If you have any doubts in a problem, you can contact us (team@opengenus.org) anytime.

Bitwise Programming is a powerful Algorithmic technique which can help you tackle critical performance optimizations.

Now on completing this book, you have conquered this core domain of Algorithm.

For more practice and contribute to Computing Community,
feel free to join our Internship Program:
internship.OPENGENUS.org